POEMS ON THE PATH

by
David McMahon

MAPLE
PUBLISHERS

POEMS ON THE PATH

Author: David McMahon

ISBN 978-1-83538-304-9 (Paperback)
978-1-83538-305-6 (E-Book)

Cover Design and Book Layout by:
White Magic Studios
www.whitemagicstudios.co.uk

Published by:
Maple Publishers
Fairbourne Drive, Atterbury,
Milton Keynes,
MK10 9RG, UK
www.maplepublishers.com

BBT Publications, Sanskrit texts, translations, and purports courtesy of the Bhaktivedanta Book Trust International, used with permission.

A CIP catalogue record for this title is available from the British Library.

DEDICATION

I dedicate this book unto all the Vaishnava devotees of the Lord. They are just like desire trees who can fulfil the desires of everyone, and they are full of compassion for the fallen conditioned souls.

ACKNOWLEDGMENTS

I would like to thank His Divine Grace A.C. Bhaktivedanta Swami Prabhupada, Founder-Ācārya of the International Society for Krishna Consciousness.

His Holiness Satsvarupa Dasa Goswami.

His Holiness Yadunandana Swami

And all the devotees and well-wishing friends who have made this book possible.

CONTENTS

Dedication 3

Acknowledgments 4

Seeking 7

A Merciful Dawn 10

Srila Prabhupada 14

Death 17

Fear 21

Morning Darshan 23

Association 25

An Inner Fiend 27

Service 30

Renunciation 34

Humility 36

Miracles 38

Simplicity 39

An Offering 42

Chanting 46

Caged Birds 48

Matrimony 50

Joy and Sorrow 52

Destiny....................55

Beauty....................58

The Factory....................61

A Loved One Lost....................65

In The Courtyard....................67

One God....................71

Forgiveness....................76

Time....................79

Progeny....................81

The Golden Nightingale....................82

Your Words....................85

A Prayer....................87

About The Author....................89

Seeking

In our very first moment..
The end of a busy week..
With the change of the seasons..
When our path becomes too steep..
At the dawning of the day..
The times we are at our peak..
When in Mother Nature's lap..
Or our most successful streak..
The start of a new chapter..
When we feel humble and meek..
Moments with our dearly loved..
When we're old, feeble, and weak..
With every new fresh breath..
The times we are in too deep..
In joining our hands to pray..
At night as we lie asleep..
It is Krishna that we seek..
It is Krishna that we seek..

Throughout life, the general tendency is to spend the majority of our time absorbed in the temporary offerings of this material world. We become so engrossed in the external happenings of everyday life that we forget to investigate or delve deeply into the real meaning of life.

Bg. 2.44

bhogaiśvarya-prasaktānāṁ
tayāpahṛta-cetasām
vyavasāyātmikā buddhiḥ
samādhau na vidhīyate

Translation

In the minds of those who are too attached to sense enjoyment and material opulence, and who are bewildered by such things, the resolute determination for devotional service to the Supreme Lord does not take place.

The temporary pleasures of this world are always calling for our attention. However, when we seek to gratify our senses, we become unnecessarily entangled and bewildered by the material energy.

Bg. 15.1

śrī-bhagavān uvāca
ūrdhva-mūlam adhaḥ-śākham
aśvatthaṁ prāhur avyayam
chandāṁsi yasya parṇāni
yas taṁ veda sa veda-vit.

Translation

The Supreme Personality of Godhead said: It is said that there is an imperishable banyan tree that has its roots upward and its branches down and whose leaves are the Vedic hymns. One who knows this tree is the knower of the Vedas.

The spiritual world is compared to a tree. And this material world is compared to a reflection of that tree on a volume of water. The material world is therefore referred to as a distorted reflection of the original spiritual world. The soul is sat cit ananda: eternal and full of knowledge and bliss. The soul is superior to the unconscious dull elements of this perverse reflection and can never become satisfied by attempting to enjoy through the medium of matter. We may try to enjoy life through the various sense pleasures available to the body, but this can never satisfy our soul or the Supreme Lord and results only in our frustration.

We are individual souls, and we have an eternal relationship with the Supreme Personality of Godhead, Lord Sri Krishna. We can therefore only be truly satisfied by acting in accordance with our original relationship as servants of the Lord. And this will enable us to find the fulfilment we all seek in our lives.

A Merciful Dawn

Of all that I had heard and all that I had seen
I have fled on a zephyr, venting my spleen
For destinies change, like the flick of a switch
I was seeking life, only truth could enrich

I realise, when I was lost and could not see
It was you who were calling, "Come home, it's me."
Deeply troubled and drifting farther away
Your voice rang clear, and I came under your sway

I was a victim of lust, anger, and greed
Krishna, your grace sprouted, my heart's inner seed
Like unaccustomed eyes, struck by shafts of light
I, in wonderment, beheld, a new world bright

I am fallen, lowly, wretched, and obscene
You, with compassion, have shown me pastures green
How can I repay you for all that's been done?
You have blessed me with life amidst the sun

Let me serve you, my Lord, and do what I can
I long to be an instrument in your plan
You are love personified, that knows no bounds
Your glories unlimited, simply astounds

I pray, please let me serve you with all my heart
I know, purity and I, are far apart
Let me remember you, Krishna, without end
You are my worshipable Lord and best friend

As we become entrapped in this material world, we naturally succumb to identifying with the body.

Bg. 3.27
prakṛteḥ kriyamāṇāni
guṇaiḥ karmāṇi sarvaśaḥ
ahaṅkāra-vimūḍhātmā
kartāham iti manyate

Translation

The spirit soul bewildered by the influence of false ego thinks himself the doer of activities that are in actuality carried out by the three modes of material nature.

Our false ego makes us think that we are the proprietors and the enjoyers of all that we survey. We think we are the body and that all our activities are our own doing. In fact, we are simply instruments of the three modes of material nature, namely, goodness, passion, and ignorance. (The three modes of material nature are elaborately described in the fourteenth chapter of the Bhagavad-Gita.)

It is these modes that keep us entrapped in this material world. When under the spell of the material modes, we are simply puppets in the hands of the Lord's illusory energy, maya. The more we become engrossed in trying to enjoy independently of the Lord, the more we become entangled and degraded by the influence of the material energy.

Bg. 7.14

daivī hy eṣā guṇa-mayī

mama māyā duratyayā

mām eva ye prapadyante

māyām etāṁ taranti te

Translation

This divine energy of Mine, consisting of the three modes of material nature, is difficult to overcome. But those who have surrendered unto Me can easily cross beyond it

The Lord's illusory energy is impossible for the conditioned souls to overcome through their own endeavour. They must seek the Lord's shelter and render service to Him. To surrender to the Lord, one must seek the shelter of His representative, the spiritual master. Then one can easily cross beyond the influence of the modes of material nature.

The three modes of material nature give the conditioned soul an illusory sense of happiness. In actuality, real happiness can only be experienced when we transcend the three modes of material nature and reach the stage of pure goodness (transcendental to the modes of material nature). This can only be achieved by following the prescribed method of the revealed scriptures.

Bg. 7.16

catur-vidhā bhajante māṁ
janāḥ su-kṛtino 'rjuna
ārto jijñāsur arthārthī
jñānī ca bharatarṣabha

Translation

O best among the Bhāratas, four kinds of pious men begin to render devotional service unto Me – the distressed, the desirer of wealth, the inquisitive, and he who is searching for knowledge of the Absolute

These are the four ways a devotee takes shelter in Krishna. When one engages in the service of the Lord, the purest aspiration is to simply try to please the Lord. Even though a devotee has a conditioned nature, they have been given the privilege of engaging in devotional service by the mercy of the Lord. By engaging in the Lord's service, one can become purified from all material contamination and awaken a transcendental loving relationship with the Lord. In this way, we can perfect our lives by becoming Krishna conscious.

Srila Prabhupada

His Divine Grace A.C. Bhaktivedanta Swami
Prabhupada
Krishna's dear devotee, a venerable Vaishnava,
saffron-clad.
He with compassion came, to save each and
every fallen soul
He preached a message of eternal truth, not
looking to cajole

He, a man in the autumn of life, was not to sit in
reserve
His spiritual master's instructions, he simply
tried to serve
With the buoyancy of youth in old age, to the
West he set sail
He struggled, he prayed, and he cried, and those
seeking truth did avail.

Born into a Vaishnava family, his life a
preparation
He was a Krishna-conscious soul in every
situation
He disseminated to the world, eternal
scriptures of old
"In every town and village" he preached,
eloquently and bold

Humble and meek, he would constantly serve,
his life a testament
A liberated soul who, on a noble mission,
Krishna sent
Always absorbed in Krishna's name, he had an
oceanic smile.
He moved with the ease of grace, a gait of
aristocratic style

He is Patita Pavana: for the fallen souls a
saviour
He made sincere hearts pure and adorned them
with saintly behaviour
Please accept my most humble obeisances, Srila
Prabhupada
Krishna's dear devotee, a venerable Vaishnava,
saffron-clad.

His Divine Grace A.C Bhaktivedanta Swami Prabhupada, is the founder Acharya of the International Society for Krishna Consciousness (ISKCON). On the order of His spiritual master Srila Bhaktisiddhanta Sarasvati Thakur, Srila Prabhupada took on the mission of spreading Krishna consciousness to countries throughout the world. In trying to please His spiritual Master, Srila Prabhupada spent the majority of His life preparing for this mammoth task. At the age of seventy he travelled to the United States of America, and began spreading the sankirtan movement of Lord Sri Chaitanya Mahaprabhu.

He has left us with the priceless treasure trove, of his translations and commentaries, in the form of scriptures such as the Bhagavad-Gita (As it is), Srimad Bhagavatam, Caitanya Caritamrta, The Nectar of Devotion, The Nectar of Instruction and The Sri Isopanisad.

He not only spread the Krishna consciousness movement throughout the world, but he laid the foundation for the future of this movement and left us with everything we need, to build a home in which the whole world can live. He has gifted us with His priceless instructions and vision, by which we can become empowered to grow in devotion and bring about true peace and happiness in today's misguided world.

This is an offering to the most munificent Srila Prabhupada.

Death

Not as dark as we may think
That unabating event
Not an untimely brink
But a happening God sent

In truth, we are eternal
For the soul can never die
Our flesh and bones external
We are bound by karmic tie

We must pass away one day
Our body is of the earth
It's aiding us on our way
As we utilise this birth

This world is a learning ground
And dying, our final test,
Always lessons to be found
For we move at God's behest

Death's a welcome stepping stone
For in settings born anew
Life's real purpose may be known
And devotion shall ensue

Krishna's hand is merciful
He wishes not to suppress
No arrangement farcical
For His sanctions are to bless

We must be weary of sin
Destiny is in our hands
Let's, with devotion, begin
And wash the past from the sands

My Lord, I will worship thee
As you are the greatest friend
Thus, embrace eternity
For in serving, there's no end

"Hundreds and thousands of living entities meet death at every moment, but a foolish living being nonetheless thinks himself deathless and does not prepare for death. This is the most amazing thing in this world."

[Mahabharata, Vana-parva 313.116]

It truly is an amazing thing; that people see death all around them, and across the different species of life, yet they fail to acknowledge this reality, and act as if it will never happen to them.

People are so bewildered with ambitions of material enjoyment that they fear death and generally do not come to terms with this reality of life. For souls imprisoned in this material world, the cycle of birth and death is

God's arrangement for their rectification and salvation. By Krishna's unlimited mercy, He gives the fallen souls chances time and again to become free from this cycle and awaken their eternal relationship with Him.

Bg. 2.13

dehino 'smin yathā dehe
kaumāraṁ yauvanaṁ jarā
tathā dehāntara-prāptir
dhīras tatra na muhyati

Translation

As the embodied soul continuously passes, in this body, from boyhood to youth to old age, the soul similarly passes into another body at death. A sober person is not bewildered by such a change.

The process of the soul passing from one body to another is known as the transmigration of the soul. To become sober means to see the world through the eyes of scriptures. Krishna has revealed everything we need to know to become free from this world. He has given us the process of Krishna consciousness and the chanting of His Holy Names: Hare Kṛṣṇa, Hare Kṛṣṇa, Kṛṣṇa Kṛṣṇa, Hare Hare/ Hare Rāma, Hare Rāma, Rāma Rāma, Hare Hare. This is known as the maha-mantra. Chanting the Lord's Names is the process recommended by the scriptures for this age, as inaugurated by Lord Sri Chaitanya Mahaprabhu.

Through the process of devotional service, we begin to identify ourselves as spiritual beings who are eternal servitors of the Lord. Thus, through the process of devotional service, we can embrace eternal life in our original constitutional position.

Bg. 18.66

sarva-dharmān parityajya
mām ekaṁ śaraṇaṁ vraja
ahaṁ tvāṁ sarva-pāpebhyo
mokṣayiṣyāmi mā śucaḥ

Translation

Abandon all varieties of religion and just surrender unto Me. I shall deliver you from all sinful reactions. Do not fear.

This is Krishna's final instruction in the Bhagavad-Gita. Just surrender unto Him and he promises to give one full protection. Therefore, we can confidently accept this promise of the Lord and give up all attachment to bodily designations by fully realising ourselves as eternal servitors of the Lord.

Fear

From a bodily conception
Fear presents itself in our life
It is due to our perception
The indwelling soul knows no strife

We must make a firm decision
To seek the truth, once and for all
Thus awaken our true vision
And amongst crashing worlds, stand tall

By nurturing a higher taste
Our perception will become clear
And if God's love, we have embraced
There is simply nothing to fear

When Srila Prabhupada was asked how he feels when he is chanting, he replied, that he feels fearless. This is what it means to be transcendently situated. It means to transcend all material affiliation. For many lives, we have been accustomed to thinking that we are this body. It is something that is so deeply ingrained in us from countless births.

In the human form of life, people are mainly preoccupied with the animal propensities of eating, sleeping, mating, and defending. This defending propensity can also be called fearing and is manifest by people seeking security in their financial circumstances and through family relations etc. When one learns to dovetail these propensities under the guidance of a bona-fide spiritual master then they can become perfect.

Bg. 18.54

brahma-bhūtaḥ prasannātmā
na śocati na kāṅkṣati
samaḥ sarveṣu bhūteṣu
mad-bhaktiṁ labhate parām

Translation

One who is thus transcendentally situated at once realizes the Supreme Brahman and becomes fully joyful. He never laments or desires to have anything. He is equally disposed toward every living entity. In that state he attains pure devotional service unto Me.

Morning Darshan

In mood of reverential awe
Bowing down as the curtains draw
Submitting to their lotus feet
Their supreme Lordships, they do greet

Meeting early under the moon
Devotion rings in blissful tune
Resounding voices all unite
Praising God in the dark of night

Standing before the Lord Supreme
Elated faces start to gleam
Thanking their master for the gift
Of deliverance, sure and swift

Not conceiving forms of this world
For their true vision has unfurled
Knowing each personality
As living form, eternally

Seeing the Lord's salient stance
With melting hearts, their eyes advance
Beheld within their Lordship's sight
Unencumbered by worldly plight

Raising their hands into the sky
Surrender sounds in soulful cry
Letting what's inside uncover
Enchanted by the soul's lover

This poem is about the first Aarti of the day, called Mangala Aarti. It takes place at four thirty each morning. At this time, devotees sing a song called Gurvastakam in honour of the spiritual master. At four thirty every morning, the curtains of the altar open, and devotees get the opportunity to have what is known as darshan of the presiding Deities.

"One who thinks the Deity in the temple to be made of wood or stone, who thinks of the spiritual master in the disciplic succession as an ordinary man, who thinks the Vaishava in the Acyuta-gotra to belong to a certain caste or creed or who thinks of caranāmrta or Ganges water as ordinary water is taken to be a resident of hell." (Padma Purāna)

The Deity form of the Lord is also known as the arca-vigraha. By the Lord's causeless mercy, He descends in this form so we can learn to serve Him properly while developing a personal relationship with Him.

Association

I once treaded in shallow depths
Naivety did lead the way
Traversing in untoward steps
Bewildered, I was led astray

Simply afraid of going deep
And attached to what seemed secure
We are the company we keep
I have come to know this, for sure

We should recognise a mere fool
Discernment comes from what they speak
And listening, the golden rule
Drawing us nearer, as we seek

We need to hear from the right source
For true knowledge has been revealed
And it's a fundamental force
In awakening, what's concealed

The Lord's devotees bestow truth
Mercifully, they rescued me
In salvaging my misspent youth
They showed me the depths of the sea

Their companionship's a great need
It is this, we must always keep
They give us the strength to proceed
And in our devotion, dive deep

As the saying goes, "You are the company you keep." This is an important principle in devotional life. In order to remain aloof from the degrading influence of the material energy, we have to remain in the association of devotees of the Lord. If you want to be like a king, walk with kings. And if we want to be fully conscious of Krishna, we should associate with Krishna-conscious people. Everything that we associate with affects our consciousness. Therefore, when we search for true knowledge, we should hear from the revealed scriptures, not knowledge that is contrived from mental speculation.

By having regular association with the devotees, we create a conducive environment for us to successfully grow in our devotion for the Lord.

An Inner Fiend

A phantom rose to seal my lips
He stalled my speech amid his clasp
And hope seemed gone—a rare eclipse
I yearned to hide, yet strove agasp
My head did simmer to a boil
Dumfounded, reddened, through the toil

The demon springing from inside
My prancing pride, he throttled down
The brute did help, I must confide
To set me free from false renown
My negligence, it gave him birth
A fault of mine, now come to hurt

And when I view the looking glass
Of trials we face, it dawns on me
These challenges we need to pass
These stumbling blocks can set us free
Yes, there's a plan for us to grow
And there's a place we ought to go

By God's grace, darkness shall subside
Devotion's light will clear the way
And within, demons shan't reside
For one who serves the Lord each day
O Krishna's name, I'll sing aloud
To serve his feet now makes me proud

The allegorical demon spoken about in this poem represents an anartha (an unwanted thing within the heart). Our hearts are full of these unwanted things. However, through the process of devotional service and with the chanting of the Lord's holy names: Hare Kṛṣṇa, Hare Kṛṣṇa, Kṛṣṇa Kṛṣṇa, Hare Hare/ Hare Rāma, Hare Rāma, Rāma Rāma, Hare Hare, one can purify their heart as they grow in their relationship with the Lord. These anarthas will naturally provide us with tests; however, no obstacle on our path is insurmountable by the mercy of the Lord. And the Lord will never give us a challenge in which we cannot succeed.

CC Antya 20.12

ceto-darpaṇa-mārjanaṁ bhava-mahā-dāvāgni-nirvāpaṇaṁ
śreyaḥ-kairava-candrikā-vitaraṇaṁ vidyā-vadhū-jīvanam
ānandāmbudhi-vardhanaṁ prati-padaṁ pūrṇāmṛtāsvādanaṁ
sarvātma-snapanaṁ paraṁ vijayate śrī-kṛṣṇa-saṅkīrtanam

Translation

"'Let there be all victory for the chanting of the holy name of Lord Kṛṣṇa, which can cleanse the mirror of the heart and stop the miseries of the blazing fire of material existence. That chanting is the waxing moon that spreads

the white lotus of good fortune for all living entities. It is the life and soul of all education. The chanting of the holy name of Kṛṣṇa expands the blissful ocean of transcendental life. It gives a cooling effect to everyone and enables one to taste full nectar at every step.'"

Service

Our foremost propensity
Comes from inside
Deep in our heart
Where the soul does reside

Forever a driving force
The cause of deeds
Seeking to find
An answer to our needs

And mistakenly, we seek
Happiness in
Material life
Where our troubles begin

We have a choice of two paths
One's full of pain
Or we can walk
The way of soulful gain

We're forever bound to serve
It is innate
Where we find joy
In our natural state

To serve is never a chore
But a pleasure
As we unearth
Our innermost treasure

The satisfaction we seek
This we can find
Through devotion
And in love, be entwined

To serve a rightful master
That is ideal
For if they're pleased
The truth they will reveal

Serving the Lord's devotees
That is the way
Of fulfilment
For their grace, we should pray

Each devotee's a servant
Of a servant.
A succession
Of love, that is fervent

The soul's nature is to render service, just as the nature of sugar is to be sweet. Due to this nature, we are always involved in some course of activity.

Bg. 4.11

ye yathā māṁ prapadyante
tāṁs tathaiva bhajāmy aham
mama vartmānuvartante
manuṣyāḥ pārtha sarvaśaḥ

Translation

As all surrender unto Me, I reward them accordingly. Everyone follows My path in all respects, O son of Pṛthā.

We are therefore either engaged in serving the Lord's internal energy (spiritual) or the Lord's external energy (material). Thus, we are either engaged in the service of our material senses or in the Lord's service. By serving the Lord, we develop our true relationship with Him and thus become purified and free from all sinful activity. And by serving our senses, we become more entangled in material life and become embroiled in sinful activities, and our consciousness naturally suffers degradation.

Bg. 4.34

tad viddhi praṇipātena
paripraśnena sevayā
upadekṣyanti te jñānaṁ
jñāninas tattva-darśinaḥ

Translation

Just try to learn the truth by approaching a spiritual master. Inquire from him submissively and render service unto him. The self-realized souls can impart knowledge unto you because they have seen the truth

The process of developing our loving relationship with the Lord and becoming free from material life involves taking shelter of the Lord's representative, the spiritual master. If we render service unto the spiritual master and hear from him submissively, he can impart true knowledge unto us. And also, by following his instructions and thus taking shelter of him, we can be led by Him to become fully cognizant of our eternal relationship with Krishna.

Renunciation

What we possess is not our own
Albeit, for now, in our care
Our misuse, God shall not condone
For Krishna's laws are always fair

With the harvest of each season
We acquire our allotted share
To forget the Lord is treason
We should be grateful in prayer

Everything belongs to Him
He is the source of all we see
It is His grace in which we swim
Our cups are filled by His mercy

We should use only what we need
And toil, simply for His favour
By living life in selfish greed,
Avid love, we shall not savour

Īśo 1

īśāvāsyam idaṁ sarvaṁ
yat kiñca jagatyāṁ jagat
tena tyaktena bhuñjīthā
mā gṛdhaḥ kasya svid dhanam

Translation

Everything animate or inanimate that is within the universe is controlled and owned by the Lord. One should therefore accept only those things necessary for himself, which are set aside as his quota, and one should not accept other things, knowing well to whom they belong.

Everything belongs to the Lord. As living entities conditioned by the influence of material energy, we have a tendency to believe that we are the controllers and proprietors of all that we survey. In actuality, everything is a gift from the Lord. We should therefore use only what is required for us to serve the Lord. This is real renunciation.

It is false renunciation if we renounce things that can be used in the service of the Lord. Srila Prabhupada was shown a picture by his disciples of a so called renunciant who was sitting beside a large sum of cash and looked disinterested. Srila Prabhupada remarked that if that were him, he would have his arms outstretched as he would use the money in the service of the Lord.

Humility

To be humble
Means to know
Who you are
And who you're not

To serve the Lord
With all your heart
Accepting fully
Your insignificance

To praise Him
And thank Him
Treating each soul
As His beloved

While you witness
His merciful hand
Throughout life's
Turning tides

CC Ādi 17.31
tṛṇād api su-nīcena
taror iva sahiṣṇunā
amāninā māna-dena
kīrtanīyaḥ sadā hariḥ

Translation

"One who thinks himself lower than the grass, who is more tolerant than a tree, and who does not expect personal honour yet is always prepared to give all respect to others can very easily always chant the holy name of the Lord."

Real humility is knowing our position in relation to the Lord and acting accordingly. Our constitutional position is that of an eternal servitor of the Lord. In this position, we find the greatest satisfaction.

And as we live a God-centred life, we see and appreciate everything in relation to the Lord. We realise that everything and everybody exists only in connection with the Lord. And we realise that all the happenings in our lives, whether they are pleasant or troublesome, are arranged by the Lord so we may grow in our relationship with Him.

Miracles

That which we behold, as miraculous to see
Is more than a show of material energy
It's a permanent change by which one becomes pure
Where all sins begin to fleet, and love does endure

The Vedic scriptures give us a deeper understanding of miracles. What is commonly understood to be a miracle is that which is beyond our limited material understanding. However, from the Vedic scriptures, we understand that yogis following the eight-fold path known as ashtanga yoga often get sidetracked by the allurement of these mystic siddhis. These siddhis allow the yogis to manipulate the material creation of the Lord. Through austerities and penances, these yogis can attain them. It should be noted, however, that the ability to manipulate matter does not mean that the yogi is pure-hearted in their devotion to the Lord.

There have been many occurrences in the past where such yogis have taken advantage of innocent people by giving demonstrations of their mystic power in order to fool them into believing that they were God. Having fooled such innocent people by producing gold, performing healings, and so on, they have been able to exploit them.

Actually, if an individual has developed the twenty-six qualities of a devotee as mentioned in the Bhagavad-Gita, that is a true sign of their saintliness. It is, however, not a sign that they are God. There are specific signs by which we can recognise God; they are also mentioned in the Vedic scriptures.

Simplicity

Simple are they
Whose intelligence
Is single-branched

They disregard
The enticement
Of material life

For they have tasted
Something sweeter
And more alluring

And they can tell
Right from wrong
And darkness from light

They hear of Krishna
Speak of Krishna
And see, only Krishna

Their single aspiration
Is to satisfy
The Lord of their hearts

Bg. 2.41

vyavasāyātmikā buddhir

ekeha kuru-nandana

bahu-śākhā hy anantāś ca

buddhayo 'vyavasāyinām

Translation

Those who are on this path are resolute in purpose, and their aim is one. O beloved child of the Kurus, the intelligence of those who are irresolute is many-branched.

Those who are on the path of devotional service are resolute in purpose, in that their only aim is to attain pure love of God. Those who are irresolute in purpose are interested in numerous material pursuits.

Bg. 10.9

mac-cittā mad-gata-prāṇā

bodhayantaḥ parasparam

kathayantaś ca māṁ nityaṁ

tuṣyanti ca ramanti ca

Translation

The thoughts of My pure devotees dwell in Me, their lives are fully devoted to My service, and they derive great satisfaction and bliss from always enlightening one another and conversing about Me

And those souls who have attained pure devotional service become completely absorbed in the Lord. In this state, everything they do is in relation to the Lord. Srila

Prabhupada has said, "Vaishnavism means simplicity," and this simplicity is the perfection of life.

The devotees of the Lord become fully satisfied and joyful in this state, wherein their body, mind, and words are fully surrendered to pleasing the Lord.

An Offering

Everywhere I see, souls in dismay
Encased in bodies, in this vast array
And illusions' influence, keeps them bound
Through untold days, as the world turns around

And every soul is precious and dear
No matter the form in which they appear
But the greatest gift is a human birth
It should be cherished for all that it's worth

For souls are meant to be joyous and free
Not to trifle in mere mundanity
Let us capitalise on this rare chance
And strive to attain our Lord's genial glance

Why not surrender all we have for Him?
And leave behind what is horrid and dim
Offering to our Lord, each single breath
We can nurture love as we conquer death

Souls in this world suffer many tribulations as they travel throughout the various species of life, birth after birth. One may be a human being in this life but may take birth as an animal in the next. This is known as the transmigration of the soul. The Padma Purana states that there are altogether eight million, four hundred thousand different species of life. And the soul takes birth among these various species to fulfil particular desires.

However, we must be careful with what we wish for, because so many needless desires can cause so much unnecessary suffering. This leads to a degradation of consciousness, and the individual soul then takes birth among the lower species of life. The human form of life is very rare. And in a human birth, the soul has greater faculties to contemplate and seek for the meaning of life. Therefore, a precious human birth should not be wasted in frivolous activities that seek to gratify the senses. As long as one is attached to sense gratification, they are entrapped in the cycle of birth, death, old age, and disease.

Bg. 9.34

man-manā bhava mad-bhakto
mad-yājī māṁ namaskuru
mām evaiṣyasi yuktvaivam
ātmānaṁ mat-parāyaṇaḥ

Translation

Engage your mind always in thinking of Me, become My devotee, offer obeisances to Me and worship Me. Being completely absorbed in Me, surely you will come to Me.

If we take the time to endeavour seriously and become Krishna conscious, then at the time of death we will be able to remember Krishna. And as we identify with ourselves as a spirit soul, that is, an eternal servitor of the Lord, we will transcend the limitations of the cycle of birth and death, and we will achieve our natural position of an eternal life of loving service. A devotee of the Lord is not interested in simply becoming liberated from the cycle of birth and death. A devotee is simply satisfied with serving the Lord in their original loving relationship.

Bg. 9.27

yat karoṣi yad aśnāsi
yaj juhoṣi dadāsi yat
yat tapasyasi kaunteya
tat kuruṣva mad-arpaṇam

Translation

Whatever you do, whatever you eat, whatever you offer or give away, and whatever austerities you perform – do that, O son of Kuntī, as an offering to Me.

The process is very simple. Whatever we do, we should do for the satisfaction of Krishna rather than the satisfaction of our own senses.

Every soul is precious to Krishna, whether it's within the body of an animal, a human being, or any other species of life. The nature of the material world is that one lifeform is food for another. This means that we have to kill to survive. However, Krishna tells us in the Bhagavad-gita:

Bg. 9.26

patraṁ puṣpaṁ phalaṁ toyaṁ
yo me bhaktyā prayacchati
tad ahaṁ bhakty-upahṛtam
aśnāmi prayatātmanaḥ

Translation

If one offers Me with love and devotion a leaf, a flower, a fruit or water, I will accept it.

If we offer Krishna those foodstuffs he accepts, which consist of a vegetarian diet, he will accept them, provided it's offered with love and devotion. Krishna does not require anything. He is self-satisfied. However, out of loving reciprocation, he allows us to offer Him foodstuffs. And when Krishna accepts our offering, the food then becomes sanctified and is known as prasadam (the Lord's mercy). Krishna gives us blessings in this way, and the sinful reactions accumulated by having to kill other living entities are nullified.

Chanting

As temptations flow in a constant stream
I cast aside each ephemeral dream
Forgetting the allurements, all around
I begin to bathe in transcendent sound

Submersing myself in His holy name
Unreserved surrender, my solemn aim
Hearing the vibration with sure intent
I humbly await a blessed advent

Setting my heart on our Lord's lotus feet
By my Guru's grace, merciful and sweet
Praying to be used in works unto Him
I slowly transcend each temporal whim

"Any person who is chanting the holy names of Krishna in course of time feels transcendental pleasure and very quickly becomes purified of all material contamination." – Srila Prabhupada

The process of salvation for this age is the chanting of the Lord's holy names: Hare Kṛṣṇa, Hare Kṛṣṇa, Kṛṣṇa Kṛṣṇa, Hare Hare/ Hare Rāma, Hare Rāma, Rāma Rāma, Hare Hare.

ŚB 12.3.51

kaler doṣa-nidhe rājann
asti hy eko mahān guṇaḥ
kīrtanād eva kṛṣṇasya
mukta-saṅgaḥ paraṁ vrajet

Translation

My dear King, although Kali-yuga is an ocean of faults, there is still one good quality about this age: Simply by chanting the Hare Kṛṣṇa mahā-mantra, one can become free from material bondage and be promoted to the transcendental kingdom.

When we chant the maha-mantra, we are asking the Lord to please engage us in His devotional service. It is a very simple process by which one can perfect their life.

Caged Birds

We are captives of our own longing
And we have hankered for something imagined
What did we see in those distant dreams?
For we now glean our own inner dearth
We have flown from where abundant hills bathe in the sun
And we have found naught but barren land
And the winds of our own fashioning
Have failed to sustain our dreary flight
And still, we cling to what we have become accustomed
Caged by the mortal whims of our destitution

Srila Prabhupada has used the analogy of a bird trapped in a cage in relation to our predicament in this material existence. The soul of the living entity has fallen from the spiritual world in order to try and enjoy separately from Krishna. However, that is not possible. In the spiritual world, we have everything we truly need. Life in this material world is troublesome and ultimately unfulfilling. Krishna is infallible; however, we minute living entities are fallible and prone to falling from the spiritual sky.

Our position in this material world is not ideal. This world is a prison house, meant for our rectification. And in this cage of material existence, we become captivated and try to enjoy an unnatural situation. However, by taking shelter of the Spiritual Master, who is Krishna's representative, we can become free from this burdensome cage by his mercy.

There is a story from scripture that tells of Lord Indra being cursed. Lord Indra is the King of Heaven. And as a result of this curse, he took birth as a hog and lived a hog life with a hog family. When Lord Brahma came to relieve Lord Indra from the abominable condition of a hog's life, Lord Indra was not inclined to give up that life. He had become attached to his hog family and hog way of life. This is our position in the material world; we become attached to lower activities, just as the hog eats stool, and this is our true poverty. We try to enjoy life through mundane sense gratification and do not seek to become self-realised as an eternal servant of the Lord.

Matrimony

As souls join, in ceremonial bind
An avowal spoken, a sacred seal
Hand in hand, with eternity in mind
And the myriad of time to reveal

They set their hearts on a love more splendid
Supporting each other with loyalty
And in devotion, all shall be mended
As they learn to serve for eternity

The purpose of married life is to help one grow in love for the Lord. There are four different stages of life in Vedic culture. First of all, there is student life (brahmachari), then there is married life (grihastha), and then there is the stage where both the husband and the wife become detached from family relations, and becoming more renounced, they focus exclusively on their devotional life (vanaprastha). And then there is the final stage of complete renunciation, which is called sannyasa. Also, one can remain a brahmachari (celibate student) for life or, from the brahmachari ashram, accept the order of sannyasa directly without going through the grihastha ashram.

Married life is not meant for sense gratification through sexual indulgence. Sexual intercourse is only meant to be had for the purpose of creating Krishna-conscious children. In married life, the man and woman should both support each other in advancing spiritually. They both have different roles that they perform, and this will lead to a happy family life as they focus on the pleasure of the Lord rather than the pleasure of their own senses. By living a life of rules and regulations in Krishna consciousness, they avoid a life that degrades their consciousness to the level of animals, but instead, their consciousness becomes purified as they strive for the perfection of love of God.

Joy and Sorrow

The pains and pleasures we meet upon our
path are temporary
Like the rise and fall of infinite waves as the
shore greets the sea
What we comprehend as joy or sorrow is a
misconception
A veil of dense darkness has blinded us from
complete perception
Trapped and tightly bound by the hard knot
of bodily attachment
From time immemorial, we've chased a
fallacy of false allurement

Inside this body is our soul, forever existing
and free
Full of bliss and knowledge, seeking
fulfilment for eternity
When our hearts become elated, steeped in
ambrosial sentiments
No more shall we be weighed down, in heed,
of evanescent events
In relation with Krishna, we can transcend all
joy and sorrow
We can live a fruitful life here and now and
with each tomorrow

Bg. 2.14

mātrā-sparśās tu kaunteya
śītoṣṇa-sukha-duḥkha-dāḥ
āgamāpāyino 'nityās
tāṁs titikṣasva bhārata

Translation

O son of Kuntī, the nonpermanent appearance of happiness and distress, and their disappearance in due course, are like the appearance and disappearance of winter and summer seasons. They arise from sense perception, O scion of Bharata, and one must learn to tolerate them without being disturbed.

The happiness and distress we experience in life is temporary. We may experience great happiness at any given time, but it is never permanent in the material world. And happiness and distress come and go like the change of the seasons. It is wise to learn the art of being able to tolerate these external changes.

Bg. 2.48

yoga-sthaḥ kuru karmāṇi
saṅgaṁ tyaktvā dhanañ-jaya
siddhy-asiddhyoḥ samo bhūtvā
samatvaṁ yoga ucyate

Translation

Perform your duty equipoised, O Arjuna, abandoning all attachment to success or failure. Such equanimity is called yoga.

Yoga means union. Real yoga is the process of connecting with God in a loving relationship. This is known as transcendental loving service. To be engaged in the devotional service of the Lord means we should strive to be unattached to the results of our service. If we aim to please Krishna, then we can overcome attachment to so-called success and failure.

Bg. 2.59

viṣayā vinivartante
nirāhārasya dehinaḥ
rasa-varjaṁ raso 'py asya
paraṁ dṛṣṭvā nivartate

Translation

Though the embodied soul may be restricted from sense enjoyment, the taste for sense objects remains. But, ceasing such engagements by experiencing a higher taste, he is fixed in consciousness.

The problem is that we are deeply attached to our material bodies. This hard knot of material attachment can be easily severed by engaging wholeheartedly in a loving devotional relationship with Lord Sri Krishna.

Destiny

What is destined for you
Has not been inscribed
By the tools of the engraver
In immutable stone

And what's been recorded
In the desert of your past
Can be made smooth
By the winds of today

And the scriptwriter
Of moments yet to come
Has dipped his pen
In the contents of your heart

Bg. 4.17
karmaṇo hy api boddhavyaṁ
boddhavyaṁ ca vikarmaṇaḥ
akarmaṇaś ca boddhavyaṁ
gahanā karmaṇo gatiḥ

Translation

The intricacies of action are very hard to understand. Therefore one should know properly what action is, what forbidden action is and what inaction is.

Karma means action. There are three different types of karma: karma, vikarma, and akarma.

Karma means pious activities. Vikarma means impious activities. Akarma means activities that transcend material nature.

An example of pious activity is a work of charity. An example of an impious activity is stealing another's property. Examples of activities that transcend pious and impious activities are impersonal meditation and devotional service.

When one takes to the process of devotional service, their karma changes. They no longer continue to receive the results of pious and impious activities, but Krishna provides them with events in their life that are tailor-made to help them advance spiritually. Also, when one takes to the process of devotional service, their karmic reactions become minimized. Krishna assures us in the Bhagavad-Gita (18.66) to surrender unto Him and not to fear, as He will deliver us from all sinful activities.

Bg. 18.63

iti te jñānam ākhyātaṁ
guhyād guhya-taraṁ mayā
vimṛśyaitad aśeṣeṇa
yathecchasi tathā kuru

Translation

Thus I have explained to you knowledge still more confidential. Deliberate on this fully, and then do what you wish to do.

We have been blessed with the ability to reason. We are therefore never bereft of free will. Actually, what we have is a minute independence to decide who we should serve: our own selfish desires or Krishna.

Bg. 4.11

ye yathā māṁ prapadyante
tāṁs tathaiva bhajāmy aham
mama vartmānuvartante
manuṣyāḥ pārtha sarvaśaḥ

Translation

As all surrender unto Me, I reward them accordingly. Everyone follows My path in all respects, O son of Pṛthā.

We have the choice to surrender unto Krishna's inferior material energy or His superior spiritual energy.

It all starts with the desires within our heart. The Lord knows our heart's desires, and He fulfils those desires. What is destined for us can change once we take to the process of devotional service and align our will with the Lord's.

Beauty

Beauty lies in the shadows
Beauty lies in the light
Beauty lies in what's awry
And beauty lies in what's right
Beauty is always there
To a greater or lesser degree
It depends on the eyes
By which you come to see
But there is a spectacle
Where beauty is unbound
It is the beauty of our Lord
A beauty most profound

Everything emanates from the Lord. The material manifestation as well as the spiritual world both emanate from Lord Sri Krishna.

Bg. 10.8

ahaṁ sarvasya prabhavo
mattaḥ sarvaṁ pravartate
iti matvā bhajante māṁ
budhā bhāva-samanvitāḥ

Translation

I am the source of all spiritual and material worlds. Everything emanates from Me. The wise who perfectly know this engage in My devotional service and worship Me with all their hearts.

Krishna is complete in all six opulences: strength, fame, wisdom, wealth, beauty and renunciation.

Each of these opulences is attractive. The word Krishna means attractive, and therefore, Krishna, the Supreme Personality of Godhead, is the all-attractive person.

Due to both the spiritual and material world's being part of Krishna's energies, they are attractive. The soul, conditioned by the false ego, becomes attracted to and entangled in Krishna's inferior material energy. The conditioned living entity therefore tries to enjoy this material world through the various species in this material existence.

Bg. 13.22

puruṣaḥ prakṛti-stho hi
bhuṅkte prakṛti-jān guṇān
kāraṇaṁ guṇa-saṅgo 'sya
sad-asad-yoni-janmasu

Translation

The living entity in material nature thus follows the ways of life, enjoying the three modes of nature. This is due to his association with that material nature. Thus he meets with good and evil among various species.

As the embodied soul reaches the human form of life, they get the opportunity to seek for the true meaning of their existence. They can thus become free from the entanglement of the material energy by taking shelter of the Lord's representative, the spiritual master.

Bg. 10.41

yad yad vibhūtimat sattvaṁ
śrīmad ūrjitam eva vā
tat tad evāvagaccha tvaṁ
mama tejo-'ṁśa-sambhavam

Translation

Know that all opulent, beautiful and glorious creations spring from but a spark of My splendor.

Through the process of devotional service, they can become free from the allurement of the Lord's external energy and develop their innate love for the Supreme Personality of Godhead. And thus they will see beauty in everything as they see it in relation to Lord Sri Krishna.

Lord Sri Krishna's personal form is so attractive that the gopis of Vrindavan chastised the creator of this material universe, Lord Brahma, because they were unable to see Krishna in the moment that they blinked.

The Factory

The factory walls, expansive and plain
The car-park full, each space in measured row
Some lonely trees, they stand amidst the rain
And round the clock, employees come and go
The machines running through each day and night
A competitive push, always their plight

And that's the way: supply must meet demand
Labouring continues, a constant chase
A firm salute, as consumers command
They toil and slog, and move. And move apace
The cause of this, an artificial need
Arising solely due to mankind's greed

Our dear Mother Earth, exploited for lust
Mercilessly ransacked by reprobates
The common man blindly follows with trust
While competition heightens among states
Different factions, concerned with their lot
Fervorous in desire, they scheme and plot

And where are faces warm with lambency?
And where is God amongst their business?
Sense gratification, their heart's decree

For temporary gain, comes endless stress
A superficial life, the only goal
And more and more distant, their joyful soul

Bg. 7.5
apareyam itas tv anyāṁ
prakṛtiṁ viddhi me parām
jīva-bhūtāṁ mahā-bāho
yayedaṁ dhāryate jagat

Translation

Besides these, O mighty-armed Arjuna, there is another, superior energy of Mine, which comprises the living entities who are exploiting the resources of this material, inferior nature.

The living entities of this world are fascinated with being the controllers and the enjoyers. They thus exploit the resources of this material nature as they try to satisfy their senses. As they endeavour to fulfil their material desires, they become more and more entangled in material life and thus more distant from the true nature of their soul. This kind of futile lifestyle is not capable of giving real satisfaction to the living entity.

As a result of this exploitation, Mother Earth becomes burdened, and conflict and division naturally arise in society due to the selfish ambition of the living entities.

Srila Prabhupada has referred to factories as hell. This is because they only bring hellish life into the world through unnatural living. Srila Prabhupada has said that factories mean destruction, and agriculture means construction. An agricultural basis for society is sustainable for the human race and is naturally harmonious with Mother Nature.

In this current consumer society, we have created endless artificial needs. If we embrace the idea of simple living and high thinking, we can have everything we need to live comfortably and sustainably.

When the resources of this material world are exploited, it creates competition between individual people and collectively on a national level between different states; thus, there is always an opportunity for war to begin.

Bg. 4.13

cātur-varṇyaṁ mayā sṛṣṭaṁ
guṇa-karma-vibhāgaśaḥ
tasya kartāram api māṁ
viddhy akartāram avyayam

Translation

According to the three modes of material nature and the work associated with them, the four divisions of human society are created by Me. And although I am the creator of this system, you should know that I am yet the non-doer, being unchangeable.

In the Bhagavad-Gita, Krishna has already given us the perfect social structure for society: Varnashrama. In this society, everyone will be engaged according to their nature. This society is perfect for facilitating the purpose of life by allowing each person to do their duty while dovetailing everything for Krishna's pleasure. This agrarian society also focuses on protecting cows and Brahmanas (saintly people). This is the only way to achieve a peaceful existence and unity throughout the world. By pleasing Krishna, everyone within society will also become satisfied, just as the different parts of the tree become nourished when one waters the root. And ultimately, when one serves Krishna and chants His holy name, Hare Kṛṣṇa, Hare Kṛṣṇa, Kṛṣṇa Kṛṣṇa, Hare Hare/ Hare Rāma, Hare Rāma, Rāma Rāma, Hare Hare, they awaken their innate love for the Lord and go back home, back to Godhead.

Bg. 5.29

bhoktāraṁ yajña-tapasāṁ
sarva-loka-maheśvaram
suhṛdaṁ sarva-bhūtānāṁ
jñātvā māṁ śāntim ṛcchati

Translation

A person in full consciousness of Me, knowing Me to be the ultimate beneficiary of all sacrifices and austerities, the Supreme Lord of all planets and demigods, and the benefactor and well-wisher of all living entities, attains peace from the pangs of material miseries.

Krishna is the goal of all sacrifice and austerity. If we do everything for Krishna's satisfaction, we can then attain true perfection individually and collectively.

A Loved One Lost

Don't sit and wither, like an autumn leaf
Don't lie and wallow in erroneous grief
Know that the path has been travelled before
By those exemplars who have reached the shore
Follow in the footsteps of those who came
The souls surrendered to the holy name

And please, take all you need, of time and space
As solace permeates you through love's embrace
O this world is certainly bittersweet
A place where souls temporarily meet
This sojourn of dismay, we must transcend
And the Lord, He beckons us, my dear friend

ŚB 3.4.23

Translation

Śrī Śukadeva Gosvāmī said: After hearing from Uddhava all about the annihilation of his friends and relatives, the learned Vidura pacified his overwhelming bereavement by dint of his transcendental knowledge.

Purport

Vidura was informed that the result of the Battle of Kuruksetra was the annihilation of his friends and relatives as well as the destruction of the Yadu dynasty and also the passing away of the Lord. All these hurled him into bereavement for the time being, but because he was highly advanced in transcendental knowledge, he was quite competent to pacify himself by enlightenment. As it is stated in Bhagavad-Gītā, due to our long association with bodily relationships, bereavement on account of the annihilation of friends and relatives is not at all astonishing, but one has to learn the art of subduing such bereavement with higher, transcendental knowledge. The talks between Uddhava and Vidura on the topic of Krsna began at sunset, and Vidura was now further advanced in knowledge due to his association with Uddhava.

In The Courtyard

In the courtyard of my heart, an evergreen does dwell
Its luscious fruits have lured me in with their spell
And perched on that tawny branch, You stand by my side
A companion and friend, in whom I may confide

In the courtyard of my heart, forever you dwell
Staying with me always, from heaven down to hell
And of each of my deeds, You keep a constant track
Not to condemn me, You just wish that I'd come back

In the courtyard of my heart, You dictate to me
You are the source of my conscience and memory
All my inspiration and knowledge come from You
You aid me on my course, be it faulty or true

The Vedas, like the Mundaka Upanisad, as well as the Śvetāśvatara Upanisad, compare the soul and the Supersoul to two friendly birds sitting on the same tree. One of the birds (the individual atomic soul) is eating the fruit of the tree, and the other bird (Krsna) is simply watching His friend. - Purport B.G. 2.22

The Vedic scripture gives us the analogy of two birds sitting on a tree to describe our individual soul and the supreme soul, the Paramatma (Supersoul). Krishna accompanies the individual soul in the material manifestation as the Paramatma. The Paramatma, or Supersoul, is Krishna as Ksirodakasayi Visnu, who has expanded into the heart of every living entity within the material universe. In this role, he simply observes the activities of the individual soul.

The individual soul and the supreme soul are of the same quality but different in quantity. An analogy is given that compares our soul to an individual drop in the ocean, which is compared to the Lord. An individual drop may have the same quality as the water in the ocean, but it can never be called the ocean. In the same way, we can never become God and remain separate individuals eternally. Krishna states this in the Bhagavad-Gita, chapter 15, text 7.

Bg. 18.61

īśvaraḥ sarva-bhūtānāṁ
hṛd-deśe 'rjuna tiṣṭhati
bhrāmayan sarva-bhūtāni
yantrārūḍhāni māyayā

Translation

The Supreme Lord is situated in everyone's heart, O Arjuna, and is directing the wanderings of all living entities, who are seated as on a machine, made of the material energy.

Our individual atomic soul is our true self. And based on our desires, the Supersoul within the heart is directing all our activities. The Lord is so merciful that he lets us fulfil whatever desires we have, even though they may not be in our best interest.

Bg. 13.23

upadraṣṭānumantā ca
bhartā bhoktā maheśvaraḥ
paramātmeti cāpy ukto
dehe 'smin puruṣaḥ paraḥ

Translation

Yet in this body there is another, a transcendental enjoyer, who is the Lord, the supreme proprietor, who exists as the overseer and permitter, and who is known as the Supersoul.

We cannot do anything without the Lord's sanction. He oversees all that we do at every moment. And he accompanies the individual soul throughout every species of life. This is the Lord's compassion. He wants us to come back to Him at every moment, but He does not force us. This is the nature of real love; real love cannot be forced. And when we awaken our innate love for the Lord, we can go back to Him.

Bg. 15.15

sarvasya cāhaṁ hṛdi sanniviṣṭo
mattaḥ smṛtir jñānam apohanaṁ ca
vedaiś ca sarvair aham eva vedyo
vedānta-kṛd veda-vid eva cāham

Translation

I am seated in everyone's heart, and from Me come remembrance, knowledge and forgetfulness. By all the Vedas, I am to be known. Indeed, I am the compiler of Vedānta, and I am the knower of the Vedas.

The Supersoul also helps us function in this material world. All our knowledge and intelligence come from the Supersoul. If we are sincere and want to reawaken our eternal loving relationship with the Lord, He will give us the necessary intelligence to enable us to come to Him. And thus, we will take shelter of His bona fide representative, the spiritual master. All the Vedic literature directs us to understand that Krishna is the Supreme Personality of Godhead. Krishna has given us full facility to realise our actual loving relationship with Him if we are simply willing.

One God

At the dawn of the day, in any given land
Those of different creeds can understand
What dissipates the darkness is known by many a name
Yet the sun, which we see, is still the same
And we can perceive its warmth and light
As it gives us sustenance and takes away the night
And those who know God and can see His ways
They know He's the same one, whom we all praise
For He shines bright, behind cloudy veils
And on each soul's voyage, remains the wind behind the sails
Yes, the Lord, we can appreciate
And rely on, in good faith
Whether you call yourself a Hindu, Christian, Muslim, or Jew
There is only one God who loves me and you

ŚB 1.2.11

vadanti tat tattva-vidas
tattvaṁ yaj jñānam advayam
brahmeti paramātmeti
bhagavān iti śabdyate

Translation

Learned transcendentalists who know the Absolute Truth call this nondual substance Brahman, Paramātmā or Bhagavān.

Brahman, also known as the impersonal Brahman, is described as the effulgence of the Supreme Lord. This is what transcendentalists perceive as the all-pervading light of the Lord. Those who attain realisation of the impersonal Brahman generally refer to the Lord as formless; this, however, is only a partial realisation of the absolute truth. The impersonalists believe that they can merge into this light and thus become God. This is actually impossible; we can never become God, and we will always remain individual living entities. We are like sparks, and Krishna is like the fire.

Bg. 15.7

mamaivāṁśo jīva-loke
jīva-bhūtaḥ sanātanaḥ
manaḥ-ṣaṣṭhānīndriyāṇi
prakṛti-sthāni karṣati

Translation

The living entities in this conditioned world are My eternal fragmental parts. Due to conditioned life, they are struggling very hard with the six senses, which include the mind.

The next stage of realisation is the Paramatma feature of the Lord. This is the Lord who resides within the hearts of all living entities and, indeed, every atom. The Yogis who meditate on the Lord within their hearts attain realisation of the Paramatma.

And those who attain Bhagavan realisation, realise Lord Sri Krishna in His original form as a person.

Śrī brahma-saṁhitā 5.1

īśvaraḥ paramaḥ kṛṣṇaḥ
sac-cid-ānanda-vigrahaḥ
anādir ādir govindaḥ
sarva-kāraṇa-kāraṇam.

Translation

Kṛṣṇa who is known as Govinda is the Supreme Godhead. He has an eternal blissful spiritual body. He is the origin of all. He has no other origin and He is the prime cause of all causes.

Krishna is the original supreme person. Krishna manifests himself in different forms to exhibit different moods. These forms include Lord Rama and Lord Narasimha, etc. These forms are still Krishna and are known as Vishnu tattva. The example given is that when the prime minister is at work, he exhibits a different mood from when he is playing with his children. Also, one dresses differently when they are in the office and when they are at home with their family. In this way, Krishna exhibits different forms, which are simply like a change of dress.

Individual living entities are Jiva tattva, and we can never become Vishnu tattva. We are eternal servitors of the Lord.

Krishna remains always as He is. We cannot fully recognise Him until the veil of illusion is dispersed. Krishna is like the sun; the sun is always there, but sometimes we cannot see it due to the clouds. We have to go beyond the clouds of illusion to be able to see the sun always, as it is.

Bg. 18.55

bhaktyā mām abhijānāti
yāvān yaś cāsmi tattvataḥ
tato māṁ tattvato jñātvā
viśate tad-anantaram

Translation

One can understand Me as I am, as the Supreme Personality of Godhead, only by devotional service. And when one is in full consciousness of Me by such devotion, he can enter into the kingdom of God.

Only through the process of devotional service can one know the Supreme Lord as He is.

The Demigods, who are deputed to different positions in the material creation, such as Lord Siva and Lord Brahma, are also servants of Krishna. Krishna is like the King, and the Demigods are like the government administrators of the King. They perform their prescribed duties on behalf of the King; however, they always remain subordinate to the King.

Bg. 18.66

sarva-dharmān parityajya
mām ekaṁ śaraṇaṁ vraja
ahaṁ tvāṁ sarva-pāpebhyo
mokṣayiṣyāmi mā śucaḥ

Translation

Abandon all varieties of religion and just surrender unto Me. I shall deliver you from all sinful reactions. Do not fear.

Krishna promises that he will deliver us if we simply surrender unto Him. The goal of all bona fide religions is to help one realise their eternal relationship as a servitor of the Lord. The soul's only designation is as a servant of the Lord; the soul does not identify as a Hindu, Christian, Muslim, or Jew.

Forgiveness

When others show you
A side more nefarious
Please summon to your countenance
The solemnity of forbearance

For they are lost
And bereft of love
Coated by clouds
And in need of the Lord

Inadvertently, they have been engaged
By the Lord's ingenuity
So you may comprehend
Your erroneous ways

And the burdens you have borne
Are mercy's mandate
To help you move beyond
Those shortcomings you harbour

For in every situation
There's a lesson to be learned
An aid in uncovering
The merit of the self

Therefore, I pray that each adversary
Be moved and reformed
By your own example
Of unrelenting forgiveness

CC Ādi 17.31
tṛṇād api su-nīcena
taror iva sahiṣṇunā
amāninā māna-dena
kīrtanīyaḥ sadā hariḥ

Translation

"One who thinks himself lower than the grass, who is more tolerant than a tree, and who does not expect personal honour yet is always prepared to give all respect to others can very easily always chant the holy name of the Lord."

Srila Prabhupada taught us that we should not hate the instruments of our karma. This means that whatever bad things happen to us because of the misdeeds of others, we should see those people simply as an instrument for our karmic reactions. We naturally reap the results of both good and bad actions that we have performed previously. These reactions reach their fruition through the agency of material nature. We experience these sufferings through our own body and mind, other living entities, and the demigods in the form of suffering experienced through nature, such as drought and famine.

All the reactions we experience are for our benefit. Krishna has arranged this material world in such a way that when we try to enjoy it, we become frustrated. He does not want us to remain here, but he wants us to realise our natural position as His eternal servitors. Therefore, this material world is designed in such a way that it inspires us to ask the deeper questions in life, such as "Why are we here?" and "What is the meaning of life?" It is better to feel compassion for those individuals who are inimical to us, as they are suffering in this material existence and are in desperate need of the higher truth of Krishna consciousness

Time

The sacred gift of time is too often squandered
In the pitiable offerings of a mundane world
We have been given an independent choice
As to how we shall spend each precious moment

This human form of life is a most rare opportunity
In which we may perceive who we truly are
And come to know, the purpose of our being
Attaining knowledge of and realisation of

Our eternal relationship with the Lord Supreme
Acting for His pleasure and becoming joyous
We can nurture our budding devotion
So that one day it shall be seen

To have begun blooming. And in that state
We'll become ready to be picked
From the fields of eternal spring
And laid to rest at the Lord's lotus feet.

In this age of Kali, we have a general lifespan of one hundred years, and it is known as the age of quarrel and hypocrisy. During this age, people in general are burdened with many different allurements and can find it difficult just to take care of the basic necessities. People of this age are very much engrossed in the modes of passion and ignorance and succumb to many bad habits.

Due to the unfortunate circumstances of this age, Lord Sri Caitanya Mahaprabhu has advented Himself as the Yuga avatar to give us the process of salvation. He has given us the simple process of chanting the holy names of the Lord. The Lord's holy name can be chanted at any time, place, or circumstance. And as we chant the Lord's holy name under the guidance of His bona fide representative, the spiritual master, we can very simply attain the goal of pure devotional service and overcome all the difficulties that arise due to Kali-yuga.

Bg. 11.32

śrī-bhagavān uvāca
kālo 'smi loka-kṣaya-kṛt pravṛddho
lokān samāhartum iha pravṛttaḥ
ṛte 'pi tvāṁ na bhaviṣyanti sarve
ye 'vasthitāḥ praty-anīkeṣu yodhāḥ

Translation

The Supreme Personality of Godhead said: Time I am, the great destroyer of the worlds, and I have come here to destroy all people. With the exception of you [the Pāṇḍavas], all the soldiers here on both sides will be slain.

Krishna explains that he is the time factor. And the time factor takes away our duration of life with every breath we take. For this reason, it is of the utmost importance that we utilise the precious time we have been given so that we may become fully Krishna-conscious.

Progeny

Born for selflessness, to be understood
Our children, they appear, for our own good
God's grand plan, as souls of the world, enjoy
For selfish aims, a child aids to destroy

In this material world, a man is naturally hankering after a woman. And a woman is naturally hankering after a man. All of the activities of material life have their origins in sexual desire. The process of begetting children is Krishna's plan to help us grow as people. When one has a child, they are naturally forced to think about the child's welfare rather than their own immediate sense gratification.

Having a child is a big responsibility. And if one is inviting a soul into this world, it is their duty to help that individual become Krishna-conscious.

The Golden Nightingale

He like a full mooned sky
Clears darkness from the eye

Guiding lost souls in the night
Showing us the path that's right

Like the nightingale sings
He, with compassion, brings

A message long lost to time
His chanting is most sublime

Lord Caitanya Mahaprabhu is the Yuga-avatar for this age of Kali. He has brought us the process for this age with the inauguration of the Sankirtan movement, which means the congregational chanting of the holy names of the Lord. The Sankirtan movement of singing and chanting the names of the Lord is the simple process by which every living being can awaken their innate love for the Lord.

Bg. 4.7

yadā yadā hi dharmasya
glānir bhavati bhārata
abhyutthānam adharmasya
tadātmānaṁ sṛjāmy aham

Translation

Whenever and wherever there is a decline in religious practice, O descendant of Bharata, and a predominant rise of irreligion – at that time I descend Myself.

Due to the rise of godlessness in this current age of Kali, Sri Caitanya Mahaprabhu has advented Himself for the salvation of the fallen conditioned souls. He is Krishna in the mood of His dearest devotee, Srimatee Radharani. He appears and shows us, by His supreme example, what it means to be a devotee. Krishna can come personally Himself, or He sends His representative for the upliftment of the fallen conditioned souls.

CC Madhya 6.242

harer nāma harer nāma
harer nāmaiva kevalam
kalau nāsty eva nāsty eva
nāsty eva gatir anyathā

Translation

"'In this age of quarrel and hypocrisy, the only means of deliverance is the chanting of the holy names of the Lord. There is no other way. There is no other way. There is no other way.'"

The chanting of the Lord's holy names is the way by which souls can easily overcome the degrading influence of this age of Kali. It is stated three times to lay emphasis on the importance of the chanting of the Lord's holy names. The chanting of the mahamantra: Hare Kṛṣṇa, Hare Kṛṣṇa, Kṛṣṇa Kṛṣṇa, Hare Hare/ Hare Rāma, Hare Rāma,

Rāma Rāma, Hare Hare is the way to become free from the tribulations of material existence. It is the process that is recommended above any other for this age because it is easily performed and awakens one to the realisation of the highest truth. Other processes are not as easy to perform and prove to be very troublesome for the aspirant who seeks the absolute truth.

ŚB 11.5.32

kṛṣṇa-varṇaṁ tviṣākṛṣṇaṁ
sāṅgopāṅgāstra-pārṣadam
yajñaiḥ saṅkīrtana-prāyair
yajanti hi su-medhasaḥ

Translation

In the Age of Kali, intelligent persons perform congregational chanting to worship the incarnation of Godhead who constantly sings the names of Kṛṣṇa. Although His complexion is not blackish, He is Kṛṣṇa Himself. He is accompanied by His associates, servants, weapons and confidential companions.

Your Words

Your words are a beacon of hope
Weighted with the staidness of love
The need of the hour, in their scope
For they come from the Lord above

The words of the spiritual master come directly from Krishna. The spiritual master is Krishna's representative and confidential servitor. The spiritual master is to be honoured as good as God because they are acting as an instrument of the Lord.

Bg. 4.34
tad viddhi praṇipātena
paripraśnena sevayā
upadekṣyanti te jñānaṁ
jñāninas tattva-darśinaḥ

Translation

Just try to learn the truth by approaching a spiritual master. Inquire from him submissively and render service unto him. The self-realized souls can impart knowledge unto you because they have seen the truth

Srila Prabhupada has stated that to make real progress in spiritual realisation, one must take shelter of a bona fide spiritual master. The spiritual master can give us instructions according to our own time, place, and circumstance to help us become fully Krishna-conscious. The spiritual master will never differ from the authority of the scriptures and the previous Ācāryas.

It was through the words of Srila Prabhupada's spiritual master, His Divine Grace Bhaktisiddhanta Saraswati Thakur, that he was able to spread the teachings of Krishna consciousness throughout the world. The words of the spiritual master are to be considered as the disciple's life and soul.

This is an offering to His Holiness, Yadunandana Swami.

A Prayer

I pray that I may let go
And my heart, that it stays true
Your mercy, may you bestow
As I live each day for you

For my immaculate soul
Hides, in the temporary
And your love will make me whole
As your mercy reigns in me

Help me to see you always
And the darkness, I will shun
May I bloom throughout my days
Like a flower in the sun

It is we who are attached to this material world. All we have to do is let go and become instruments of our spiritual master and Krishna. It is by the mercy of Krishna and His devotees that we can sever this attachment. Through the process of Krishna consciousness, which entails following the four regulative principles of no intoxication, no consumption of meat, fish, or eggs, no illicit sex, and no gambling, and chanting sixteen rounds a day of the Hare Krishna mahamantra, we can easily overcome the influence of material nature. This process is simple and joyful and is easily maintained with the association of devotees. Ideally, one should also attend the daily morning programme at the temple.

Srila Prabhupada stated that he would pray regularly so that he would not fall down from his transcendental position as a servitor of the Lord. We should also seek the mercy of Krishna and His devotees so that we can remain firmly situated in devotional service.

There are many examples of pure devotees who are only seeking pure devotional service. As sincere devotees, this should also be our goal. As we follow the process of devotional service, we can also pray to Krishna and His devotees for spiritual strength so that we do not let the material desires that lurk in our hearts dictate our course of action. To be desireless means to have only Krishna-conscious desires.

The bhakti-lata-bija is the creeper of devotional service within our hearts. Through the process of devotional service, we can water this creeper so that it grows and blooms in the full maturity of pure devotional service.

CC Madhya 19.167

anyābhilāṣitā-śūnyaṁ
jñāna-karmādy-anāvṛtam
ānukūlyena kṛṣṇānu-
śīlanaṁ bhaktir uttamā

Translation

'When first-class devotional service develops, one must be devoid of all material desires, knowledge obtained by monistic philosophy, and fruitive action. The devotee must constantly serve Kṛṣṇa favorably, as Kṛṣṇa desires.'

ABOUT THE AUTHOR

My name is David McMahon. As a devotee on the path of Krishna consciousness, I have been inspired to share the teachings with others and have naturally gravitated towards expressing the scriptures through poetry. I hope that this collection may encourage people to read and study the books of Srila Prabhupada and ultimately take to the path of devotional service and the chanting of the Lord's holy names.

www.ingramcontent.com/pod-product-compliance
Lightning Source LLC
Chambersburg PA
CBHW070317120526
44590CB00017B/2715
* 9 7 8 1 8 3 5 3 8 3 0 4 9 *